Titles by Janvier Chouteu-Chando

The Usurper: and Other Stories
Triple Agent, Double Cross
Disciples of Fortune
The Union Moujik
Splendid Comets
Flash of the Sun
Fortune Calls
Fortune's Master
Fortune's Children
The Norilsk Bears
To Be In Love and To Be Wise
The Fire and Ice Legend
The Sweetest Madness
The Grandmothers
The Hunger Fire
The Shades of Fire
Father and Sons
The Doctors
Dark Shades
Fateful Ties
The Verdict of Hades
His Majesty's Trial
Ngoko's Folly
The Usurper
The Dowry
I am Hated
The Oaf

Non-Fiction Titles by Janvier Chouteu-Chando

FALLEN HEROES: African Leaders Whose Assassinations…
BROKEN ENGAGEMENT: Why a Donald Trump Win…
THEIR LAST STAND: Donald Trump's Upset Victory…
Ukraine: The Tug-of-war between Russia and the West
THE CANARY IN A COAL MINE EFFECT:…
Cameroon: The Haunted Heart of Africa

Why Cameroon Needs a Fundamental Change

Janvier Tchouteu

TISI BOOKS

NEW YORK, RALEIGH, LONDON, AMSTERDAM

PUBLISHED BY TISI BOOKS
www.tisibooks.com

PUBLISHED BY TISI BOOKS
www.tisibooks.com

NEW YORK, RALEIGH, LONDON, AMSTERDAM

Printed in The United States of America

EPIGRAPH

"The time for revolutionaries with the complete freedom to maneuver is over."
   —CHRISTOPHER NKWAYEP-CHANDO

Acknowledgement

My deepest, warmest and everlasting thanks to Dr. Samuel F. Tchwenko and Christopher N. Chando for challenging me towards the path of humanity's enhancement.

DEDICATION

Dedicated to the loving memory of Dr. Mrs. Elizabeth Matsidiso Tchwenko née Chitja

Why Cameroon Needs a Fundamental Change

Contents

Quotes

"We find that at present the human race is divided into one wise man, nine knaves, and ninety fools out of every hundred. That is, by an optimistic observer. The nine knaves assemble themselves under the banner of the most knavish among them, and become 'politicians'; the wise man stands out, because he knows himself to be hopelessly outnumbered, and devotes himself to poetry, mathematics, or philosophy; while the ninety fools plod off under the banners of the nine villains, according to fancy, into the labyrinths of chicanery, malice and warfare. It is pleasant to have command, observes Sancho Panza, even over a flock of sheep, and that is why the politicians raise their banners. It is, moreover, the same thing for the sheep whatever the banner. If it is democracy, then the nine knaves will become members of parliament; if fascism, they will become party leaders; if communism, commissars. Nothing will be different, except the name. The fools will be still fools, the knaves still leaders, the results still exploitation. As for the wise man, his lot will be much the same under any ideology. Under democracy he will be encouraged to starve to death in a garret, under fascism he will be put in a concentration camp, under communism he will be liquidated."

T.H. White

"Cameroon is not a country of slaves that no man can free."
Janvier Chouteu-Chando

"Every great cause begins as a movement, becomes a business, and eventually degenerates into a racket."
Eric Hoffer

"However [political parties] may now and then answer popular ends, they are likely in the course of time and things, to become potent engines, by which cunning, ambitious, and unprincipled men will be enabled to subvert the power of the people and to usurp for themselves the reins of government, destroying afterwards the very engines which have lifted them to unjust dominion."
George Washington

"You see these dictators on their pedestals, surrounded by the bayonets of their soldiers and the truncheons of their police ... yet in their hearts there is unspoken fear. They are afraid of words and thoughts: words spoken abroad, thoughts stirring at home -- all the more powerful because forbidden -- terrify them. A little mouse of thought appears in the room, and even the mightiest potentates are thrown into panic."
Winston S. Churchill

"We are not involved in this struggle only because we think that we will dismantle this system in the course of our life. We hope that Cameroon will change tomorrow. But if not, we will be happy to know that we made fertile ground for the next generation that will end rot in this country, and then establish CAMEROON NEW. "
Dr. Samuel F. Tchwenko, former UPCist and chief ideologue of the historic SDF of 1990-2002

"These divisions, which the colonial powers have always exploited the better to dominate us, have played an important role—and are still playing that role—in the suicide of Africa."
Patrice Lumumba

"The enemy is not the one who is facing you with a sword in hand, that's the opponent. The enemy is the one behind you with a knife at your back."
Thomas Sankara

We know that Africa is neither French, nor British, nor American, nor Russian, that it is African. We know the objects of the West. Yesterday they divided us on the level of a tribe, clan and village...They want to create antagonistic blocs, satellites..."
Patrice Lumumba

"I never minded flying cheap. I always said to myself, 'Taking this flight saves enough money to rescue four dogs, or six cats, or will let me make a difference to the one woman saving chimps in Cameroon.'"
Elayne Boosler

"The greatest difficulty we have faced is the neocolonial way of thinking that exists in this country. We were colonized by a country, France, that left us with certain habits. For us, being successful in life, being happy, meant trying to live as they do in France, like the richest of the French."
Thomas Sankara

"...The world gets blessed every now and then with unique souls who though burdened by their invisible crosses, still have the extraordinary strength to forge ahead in life and give others a helping hand at the same time. Despite their tribulations, most of us think they are fine. Even when the weight of their crosses become unbearable, even when they proceed in a breathless manner, we still have a hard time understanding that they are drowning. In fact, we even condemn them for failing to sacrifice more..."

Janvier Chouteu-Chando, Disciples of Fortune

"Political independence has no meaning if it is not accompanied by rapid economic and social development."

Patrice Lumumba

INTRODUCTION

The cause for change being pursued today by the majority of Cameroonians (the struggling masses) does not bear its origins from the wind of change (demands for democracy) that Soviet leader Mikhail Sergeivich Gorbachev's Glasnost and Perestroika generated across the world, a wind of change that jolted those political systems that were failing to conform to the demands of world civilization and progress, which place the freedom and liberty of man and the interest of humanity above the twisted interest of the unscrupulous selfish minority.

The cause for change otherwise known as the Cameroonian (Kamerunian) Struggle began in 1910 led by Martin Paul Samba (Mebene Mebongo). Patriotic Cameroonians, who accept one another irrespective of their compatriots' ethnic, racial, religious or regional origins, acknowledge the fact that the first phase of the Kamerunian (Cameroonian) struggle was defeated in 1914 by the German colonial army following the execution of Martin Paul Samba and Rudolf Duala Manga Bell. They also accept the fact that because of that defeat, the land lost a unifying patriotic or civic-nationalist force to ensure Kamerun's unity during and after the First World War (The Great War), a void that played against the Kamerunian people when the victorious British and French colonial powers went about partitioning the defeated German Kamerun after the war.

The lethargy that followed the first defeat of the

Kamerunian struggle and the resultant partition of the pre-1911 German Kamerun into French Cameroun and British Cameroons (British Northern Cameroons and British Southern Cameroons) lasted for thirty years, or the equivalent of a generation, before the divided Kamerunian people revived their national consciousness again. This time around, the revival of the original objectives of the Kamerunian struggle—independence, freedom, justice, development, unity, peace, democracy, liberty, progress, international cooperation and international fraternity—was done with an additional objective of reuniting a land and a people who through no fault of theirs had been separated from one another to suit the interest of Britain, France and other foreign powers.

Reuniting Kamerunians also meant mitigating the consequences of partition and putting the land and its people on the path to realize the original purpose of the Kamerunian struggle embodied in the words "THE KAMERUNIAN DREAM" (CAMEROONIAN DREAM). This second phase of the Kamerunian struggle dominated by the quest for reunification of British Cameroons and French Cameroun was led by the UPC (*Union des Populations du Cameroun"*, otherwise known as the Union of the Populations of the Cameroons), a legal political party born in French Cameroun on April 11, 1948. The UPC and its affiliate political parties commanded more than 90% of the support of educated Cameroonians in both French Cameroun and British Cameroons and had the open or tacit backing or sympathy of more than 80% of British Cameroonians and French Camerounians before the vindictive and fearful French authorities banned the UPC on July 13, 1955, a move that was backed two years later by the British authorities in British Cameroons when the authorities there also banned the UPC in 1957. With the elimination from the political scene of the party that was the land's most dominant movement and that was the best reflection of the aspirations of the Cameroonian people, advocates for reunification and independence for the lands of the former German Kamerun(British Cameroons &French Cameroun) were in a predicament.

The fact that the UPC was left after its ban with no other option to freely lead the struggling "Kamerunian Masses" to their aspirations, the fact that the colonial powers perceived the UPC as an obstacle in their design and influence over the former German Kamerun, and the fact that its members were being hounded and killed, the UPC finally came to a conclusion that it had no other option but to resort to the path of armed resistance. The painful decision that led to more than ten years of armed resistance contributed enormously in the political evolution of the territories of the former German Kamerun and the partial reunification of these territories (British Southern Cameroons and French Cameroun), but it came about with the death of more than half a million Cameroonians (10% of the population), and it came about with the loss of British Northern Cameroons to Nigeria. Yes, the cause that spurred the fight for Cameroon's reunification and independence resulted in the reunification of British Southern Cameroons and the Republic of Cameroon (the former French Cameroon) in 1961, following the plebiscite results in British Southern Cameroons, but the price paid in achieving that was very high indeed—Cameroonians witnessed the first case of crimes against humanity committed by the French Army in French Cameroun and the puppet regime they put in place there after they made French Cameroun a member of the United Nations Organization on January 01, 1960 by granting it independence in a process that effectively made the territory a neocolonial possession of France.

The assassination of the Ruben Um Nyobe (The UPC's leader) on 13 September 1958 by French forces; the poisoning of his successor Felix-Roland Moumié in Geneva in October 1960 by the William Bechtel, an agent of the French secret service; and the execution of the third historic UPC leader Ernest Ouandié in January 15, 1971, after he gave himself up in August 1970; marked the second defeat of the Kamerunian struggle, the successful entrenchment of the French-imposed system under the regime of French puppet Ahmadou Ahidjo (the first Cameroonian president), and a new reality of a pseudo-independence to soothe the pains and emotions of the patriotic struggling Cameroonian masses and to neutralize their civic-nationalism, a very peculiar union-nationalism also called Kamerunism, which is considered an advanced ideal that brings diverse peoples together in a continent plagued by ethnic, religious and racial divisions. The carrot and stick strategy of suppression, intimidation, handouts, extortion, bribery and corruption that the French political leadership under the umbrella of FrancAfrique (France's special relationship with its former African colonies and territories established before it granted them independence) sustained the 24-year rule of Ahmadou Ahidjo, and has been sustaining the usurper regime of Ahidjo's successor Paul Biya ever since he was handed power by Ahmadou Ahidjo in 1982.

That defeat of the second phase of the Cameroonian struggle led to a second political lethargy that even saw the democratic nature of the former British Cameroons undermined after Cameroon's reunification, a process of subjugation that kept the dynamic Cameroonian people docile or politically subdued for two decades.

Today, we are in the third and hopefully or certainly the last phase of the Cameroonian Struggle to realize the Kamerunian Dream of "THE NEW CAMEROON".

That the struggling Cameroonian masses have been whisked off their political lethargy is glaring for all to see; that their determination to realize the objectives of the eight-decade old Kamerunian(Cameroonian) struggle is clearly and resolutely challenged or resisted by the status quo or the Biya regime and its external backers (The French- politically setup in Africa otherwise known as FrancAfrique) that have been benefitting from the mafia setup called the Cameroonian system, is something the world knows about. But exponents of change in Cameroon know that getting rid of the anachronistic French-imposed system is the only recourse which would allow Cameroonians to build "The New Cameroon" that would involve Cameroonians of all ethnic groups, religions, political affiliations, regions and races in the process of nation-building. Cameroonians know that getting rid of the system is the first step in reconciling Cameroon and Cameroonians.

In power since 1982 is Africa's absentee dictator Paul Biya, who was made the successor of his predecessor Ahmadou Ahidjo by an order from former French President Francoise Mitterrand; Ahidjo, who himself was brought to power by the French to usurp the aspirations of Cameroonians in their liberation struggle led by the UPC that the French banned in 1955, a party with more than 80% of the land's intellectuals and even more national support. France had made sure Ahidjo's power was secured by decimating its support base in a 12-year war against the party and by killing all the UPC leaders (Un Nyobe 1958, Felix Moumie in Geneva 1960, Ossende Ofana 1966, Ernest Ouandie 1971 etc.), leaving Cameroon a nation haunted by an "Unfinished Liberation Struggle". Today, Cameroonians are out not only to get rid of the Dictator Biya's autocracy, but also to get rid of the French-imposed system that its custodians want to continue with someone else after Paul Biya departs.

Chapter One

Cameroon is in its last stages of decay. There are no prospects of it getting out of its lethal malady by using the human and material resources that the present anachronistic system can mobilize unless the system is fundamentally changed or overthrown and a reformed or new system put in place. The first aspect of change prescribes radical reforms while the second aspect of change   requires a revolution. The first aspect calls for the replacement of most of our old and unworkable structures and values with new ones, while the second rejects all aspects of the anachronistic system and its values and calls for their total, complete and universal replacement by new ones. The difference in the two aspects of change lies only in the degree of replacement. However, the reformatory and revolutionary ideals and actions are meant to solve the socio-economic   and   political   ills   afflicting   the Cameroonian state by challenging the status quo and its formulations.

In order to challenge the status quo, exponents of change ought to be backed up by a careful study to determine whether the six-decade-old system's degree of decay would require reformatory or revolutionary measures. Well, Cameroon is rotten enough as highlighted below:

1) Cameroon's decay is wrapped up in the injustices whose resultant shortcomings now haunt our everyday lives. These injustices are in the economic, social, ethnic and political domains.

- <u>Economically</u>, Cameroon has been reduced to a beggar nation; the pride of its citizens denigrated, their dreams dashed and their hopes made to look like illusions. Yes, we are beggars despite our fabulous human and material potentials. Though having never been really rich, our fairly considerable economic standards that stood out during German colonial rule, that was exemplified in the 1950s and made remarkable between 1974-1984 (despite all the past constraints from the system and its puppet Ahidjo regime), have been greatly reduced, plunging us into abject poverty. The poverty is so deep that the vast majority of Cameroonians have lost faith in the system, the enthusiasm to engage in long-term projects to rise out of their miseries, and the dignity that befits a progressive people with a sense of purpose. The present system has made it extremely difficult for hard working and intelligent lads to rise up to their potentials, unless they compromise their honor by selling their souls for the favors from the custodians of the system, an opportunity which only a decimal are privileged to be exposed to. Government planning (both strategic and tactical) is so unrealistic, chaotic, unfocused and devoid of follow-up mechanisms that they tend to destroy and depress, instead of constructing and building resolve. There is blatant discrimination by officials at the upper echelons of the system who bog down the business and constructive efforts of the struggling masses because they are of the opposite political thinking, undesirable ethnic group or tribe, different religious belief, the hated social grouping or threatening region, or stereo-typed linguistic entity; just because these custodians of the system believe these enlightened Cameroonians threaten the status quo. Our material resources are being irrationally and wantonly exploited without an effectual development of the land and improvement in the lives of Cameroonians. Despite Cameroon's vast agricultural, mineral, energy and other natural resources, we have failed to build the base of a processing or industrial nation, so that primary commodities are the only things we export today. The pro-French political and business class and their collaborators are solely responsible for this rape of the Cameroonian nation. So far, prospects of an economic recovery still remain nil because the anachronistic system does not want to loosen the control put in place by its neo-colonialist French lords, corrupt bureaucrats, unpatriotic political elite and business class who know or care little about Cameroon's economic reality. The only way for the Cameroonian economy to stand on its feet again and assume the path of a progressive future is through a buildup of business confidence. That confidence can only be built after we rid the nation of all aspects of the economic shortcomings of the anachronistic system. Such a revolutionary task requires a rational economic transformation geared towards economic growth, transparency, a mitigation of the effects of unemployment and a commitment to involve all Cameroonians in the process of nation building.

- On the <u>social</u> scene, our Cameroon, which we hold so dearly at heart, has also not been spared of decay. Education, which is supposed to be the right of every child, has been relegated to the point of abandonment by the Biya regime. That is why today, the majority of our children are poorly educated in an academic system that is not geared towards development and rational professionalism. Our educational system is behind the times in infrastructure, equipment, knowledge, skills, and experience. The cost of educating a child has risen far above the means of the average Cameroonian due to the government's nonchalant attitude towards the granting of subsidies to schools. Today, books and other educational materials are either in short supply, unavailable or are too expensive. The majority of our teachers are poorly trained, and they and lag behind their counterparts elsewhere in the world in knowledge and skills. The undesirable result has been Cameroon's continuously falling literacy rate and the decreasing competitiveness of our graduates. Meanwhile, the children of the oligarchy and collaborators of the system pursue their education abroad. They often return as overlords with no work experience abroad, but with the professionalism to steal in a smoother manner.

- Today, hardly half a decade into the next millennium, the vast majority of the Cameroonian people are still living in filth and squalor. Good housing, available medical facilities and other social infrastructures are in short supply, having been relegated to the government's bottom list of priorities. Town planning has become so chaotic. Even the basic necessity of water and electricity are inadequately provided despite our vast potentials in those resources. In the towns and cities especially, the once noble Cameroonian people are compelled to live alongside untreated garbage dumps, giant rats, cockroaches and other vermin. The country's sanitation has fallen below pre-independence level. Even its transportation network and other infrastructures are a mockery to a people who are considered imaginative, dynamic and proud. These retrogressions are testaments to the fact that the country has fallen behind other nations since independence. In the world of advanced services and communication, the senseless system has made the country to lag pathetically behind time, even as other governments of the world quickly embrace technological progress. It does not bother the Biya regime that Cameroonians are living in misery because he has detached himself from the general Cameroonian reality and carved out a cocoon of affluence for himself and his mafia clique.

- <u>Leadership</u> over the forces that should give Cameroon its strength (The people) has been undermined by government-instigated discrimination. Clannishness, tribalism, ethno-centrism, regionalism and other forms of division are often set aflame on groups (as scapegoats) in order to dispel discontent directed against the government and the system. The regrettable outcome of such moves has been the open and latent distrust that has caused the breakdown of cooperation between the forces that are supposed to work together to realize our potentials. While it is true that the Ahidjo and Biya regimes have favored certain social groupings, especially their ethnic groups, the reproach for complicity should not be put on any ethnic or linguistic group because collaborators of the system have been bred from virtually every group in Cameroon.

2) The unavoidable consequences of the economic, social and ethnic injustices are the poor management that stand as Cameroon's chronic malady today. Due to the fact that the government's economic policies basically favor only a small minority of individuals, ethnic groups and regions; the vast potentials of the majority and disfavored are either cruelly exploited, left untapped and/or neglected. The regrettable result is that these majority and disfavored produce without a corresponding development in their lives and the environment around which they operate. This situation prevails while the favored minority swims in splendor, abundance, arrogance and mismanagement. The visible result is the inefficient utilization of our resources through over-exploitation, without the necessary subsequent developments in building and restoration. The consequence of this poorly targeted policy is the disorientation, disillusion, despondence and despair syndrome that has eaten deep into the ranks of the creative and progressive forces of the land. The fact that these forces have been estranged from participating in the running of the economic, social and political affairs of the land draws open a phase of conflict in our development—that is, how do we restore the harmonious cooperation between the political establishment and the majority of the economic sector whose advanced business leadership wants to realize a developed and progressive Cameroon? Unfortunately, for Cameroon, the majority that constitutes the creative and progressive forces are too dazed in their inability to mount a strong opposition or resistance to the system, while the minority that constitute the custodians of the system are so vocal and aggressive despite their poor records of incompetence, mismanagement, unaccountability, corruption, buffoonery, repression, waste and misuse of our resources. Unless we get rid of the management problem through the ideals of

our union-nationalism, there will never be a correction of the injustices persisting in our social, economic and inter-ethnic lives. For that to be realized, we must get rid of the anachronistic system now and fast.

3) The mismanagement in Cameroon and the injustices that are prevailing stem from its anachronistic political structure. Early in the twentieth century 1910), Cameroon's first nationalists led by Martin Paul Samba (Mebenga Mebono) and Rudolf Duala Manga Bell perceived that while striving for Kamerun's independence from Germany, its colonial master at the time, so that the land could exist within the frame work of international cooperation, they wanted the land's human and vast material resources to be rationally exploited and developed through the best combinations of internal and external cooperation. We were unfortunate because the German colonial administration opposed that new Kamerunian force. They executed its leaders, a sad epoch in our nationalism that made it to become dormant for decades, so that even after the defeat of the Germans, there was no nationalist force to defend the land against partition by the British and the French. Instead of the independence that Cameroon's first nationalists strove for, the land and the noble Kamerunian people became subservient subjects instead of the British and French in 1918. However, three decades after, there was a resurgence of Cameroonian nationalism, which garbed the extra cloths of unification and independence. While espousing the ideals of Martin Paul Samba, Rudolf Manga Bell and the other early nationalists as far back as 1946, Cameroon's union-nationalists decried the divisive, suppressive, oppressive, retrogressive and exploitative rule of its masters, specifically France and demanded the reunification and independence of the British Cameroons and French

Cameroun. Unfortunately the new masters, especially France, did not heed such a good-intentioned and authentic demand from the majority of Cameroonians. The UPC (Union of the Populations of Cameroon) that was at the forefront of the resurgent nationalism suddenly found itself tagged as communists and as an enemy of France, Britain and the western world. Using wanton oppression, the French banned the party, and then massacred, sidelined, cowed, corrupted and banished the true union-nationalists within the UPC. In the place of the union-nationalists and their original ideals, they put the French-puppet regime under Ahidjo Ahmadou to lead French Cameroun through quasi independence and reunification with British Cameroons.

It has been proven from the experiences of the past years that the majority of Cameroonians have always rejected the system and the Ahidjo and Biya regimes that the system created. Ahidjo and Biya failed to offer alternative ideas or programs on how to manage our material and human resources in order to eliminate the injustices that are plaguing Cameroon. Instead, they have shown their determination to continue defending the anachronistic system because it serves their interest to do so. The present French-backed regime relies heavily on the nation's stereotypical armed forces and secret service, just like its predecessor did. It has not been less enthusiastic about using force to quell any form of protest or drive towards genuine democracy. Being used alongside force are the various methods of intimidation, corruption, election rigging and blackmail that have proven to be effective in other places in defeating exponents of change. Completely detached from the Cameroonian people and reality, the present French-created political structure gives the president limitless powers, while retaining power and decision making at all levels with the president and his close collaborators. The results from the workings of the system and its structures are all negative, with corruption having been elevated to the form of an art and falsity having become the modus operandi of the Biya regime. The repercussions from those negative values are the pathetically deep fall in our standards, and the erosion of our hope and dignity. Still, it does not bother the Biya regime that the hopeless nature of the status quo has revealed the unworkable nature of the system and its structures. The levers of the oppressive machinery of this system are preventing any adoption or acceptance of counter measures to the regime's policies, measures that can rejuvenate the nation. That is why Cameroon's present political power (The system) must be totally, completely and irrevocably overhauled if we must find a solution to the problems of mismanagement and injustices.

4) An agonizing fall in our basic human values is the depressing outcome of the anti-people policies and governance of the system for over half a century now. The fall is also the consequence of poor management whose results are the economic, social and ethnic injustices haunting the Cameroonian nation today. Morality and its higher order of humanism, which are supposed to be the cornerstone of any prosperous nation's order, reputation, legality and even virtue, have no place in the workings of the anachronistic system and its custodian, the Biya regime. There is a breakdown in progressive family values—a rise in the rate of prostitution, drunkenness, drug abuse, juvenile delinquency and violent crime. Dishonesty and banditry have become a plague in our everyday lives. Religion has lost its original worth in the eyes of Cameroonians. What we have in place instead is the individualistic and self-centered concept of "Everyone for his/her belly", a concept that embodies corruption,

discrimination and dishonesty— ills that are haunting us today. For now, preparations and practical actions should be taken to restore the honor, dignity and progressive values of our traditions. Our new philosophy should promote constructive dialogue, cooperation and criticism. Our literature, history and other fields of art should reflect progressive and all-embracing Cameroonian values like our union-nationalism, while taking precautions to integrate only those foreign values that are compatible with Cameroonian reality. Culture, the culture that gives a nation its special identity is dying in Cameroon. With ties to virtually all the different cultural groups and language families in Africa, Cameroon deserves to be the champion of the African culture. Despite that fact, we observe today that our education, social programs, information and culture and communication actually discourage the development of our cultures. That is unacceptable.

The idea of how Cameroon should evolve as it is being experimented by the French-backed system that is under Paul Biya today has nothing progressive to offer. It has brought conformity only in the wrong values of dishonesty, corruption, disloyalty, laziness, discrimination and docility. It has failed to seek, harness and work on individual and group considerations which if put together constitute the Cameroonian view. The present out-dated system constrains us to the point of despondence, and poses as a tremendous obstacle to the development of individual and group potentials. It is almost eradicating self-identity to be replaced by a conformity based on resignation, dishonesty, corruption and brutality.

Only through a carefully thought out new value, one that realizes the best of our creative and developmental potentials and one that advocates for a fundamental change of the anachronistic system, can our potentially great nation be saved. That new value should be capable of coming up with a new culture that embodies the progressive Cameroonian cultures. It should be a culture that would help in the formulation of a progressive political structure where the powers emanating from its levers would be capable of responding to the progressive ideas and the hopes and dreams of the Cameroonian people. It is only through that reconstituted and optimally progressive political and power structure that there can be an efficient management of our human and material resources, while taking into account Cameroonian and world realities. As a consequence the economic, political, social and ethnic injustices that are prevailing due to the poor management (abuse of political power, unrealistic culture and the imposed conformity) would be properly tackled.

Today, the forces that stand as the best champion of the fundamental change are the union-nationalists. They are found in some of the political parties, religious bodies, social groupings, and also as individuals. However, in order to realize the fundamental change, our union-nationalists, young and old, would be led by the advanced representatives—the tested force.

Janvier Tchouteu   *April 4, 1995*

Chapter Two

A specter looms in the lives of every Cameroonian child, man or woman. It is the living president of the land in the middle of Africa, the land that is often referred to as the microcosm of the continent. The specter is President Paul Biya of Cameroon. When rumors spread like wildfire in June 2004 that he had just died, there were widespread scenes of jubilation all across the half a million square kilometer landmass called Cameroon. Days after the circulation of the unverified account, he returned home from abroad where he had been passing his time, intermittently, about six months every year for over two decades, and then declared to the sycophants waiting to receive him at the airport that there would be a …. "Rendez-vous in 20 years' time with those who wish me dead…"

Cameroonians were not the only ones who disbelieved him when he made that pronouncement among other things. Many of those who follow political developments in the world in general, and in Africa and Cameroon in particular, marveled at his audacity. After all, more than 80% of the Cameroonian population loathed his rule; he was already in power for more than two decades as the head of state, after having been the country's prime minister (1972-1982) or the second most powerful person in the system put in place in Cameroon by the French overlords.

But Paul Biya proved everyone wrong. He pulled off another electoral charade and declared himself the winner in the October

2004 presidential election, and then changed his constitution in 2008 that would allow him to run for two more presidential 7-year terms (despite the deaths of 150 protesting Cameroonians caused by his armed forces), meaning that he could be president until the year 2025 (a record of 43 years in power) when he would be 92 years of age.

That explains why by the time Paul Biya held another masquerade called presidential elections in October 2011, he had already successfully humbled the internationally recognized opposition heads (who are all former members of the country's sole political party from 1972-1990, a party Biya has been leading since 1984), promised to give them positions in his government and made it known in plain terms that the system string-controlled by the puppeteer (France) would never allow political change in Cameroon that would curtail France's unrestricted interests in the African country.

The octogenarian Paul Biya is variously described as the Maradona (he fakes and wins elections just like Maradona faked and scored a goal in his "Hand of God" goal) of Cameroonian and African politics, the master of presidential patricide (he devoured his predecessor who passed over power to him, leading to the first Cameroonian president Ahmadou Ahidjo's exile, death and burial abroad—Senegal), the absentee president, the vindictive president, the evil president, etc. etc.

As a German colony from 1884-1916, Kamerun was often referred to by the German Colonial administration and the imperial-minded in the Kaiser's Germany as an "African Pearl", owing to the colony's robust economy, highest literacy rate in the continent in the early 1900s, magnificent physical features, rich and varied vegetation cover, and also owing to its diverse ethnic ethnicities that included all the major language groups in Africa (Afro-Asia, Niger-Congo-A, Niger-Congo-B or Bantu, and Nilo-Saharan. in fact, historians consider the German colony of Kamerun as a major part of Adolf Hitler's rue over the territories Germany lost after the First World because of the peace terms imposed on it by the victories Allied Powers during the Versailles Conference. As it happens, one of the peace terms imposed on the post-Kaiser Germany was the loss of German Kamerun to Britain and France. That was how Kamerun was partitioned into British Cameroons and French Cameroon.

As a matter of fact, the French Cameroun mandate became France's most valuable assert in Sub-Saharan Africa. Its value was validated even further when the territory became the Launch pad of French General Charles De Gaulle-led Free French Forces that wrestled French Equatorial Africa from the Nazi puppet regime of Vichy France during the Second World War. This force would gallantly fight alongside Allied Forces against Italian and German forces in Libya, Tunisia and the Middle East, before carrying on to Italy and France where their biggest achievement was the liberation of Paris. The fact that French Camerounians played an invaluable role in the war effort to liberate France from Nazi Germany makes the explanation simple as to why French Camerounian soldiers returned home and sought self-government, liberty, democracy, reunification with British Cameroons that would culminate in the independence of the two United Nations Trust Territories. They were merely seeking the rights that they had helped France to regain from Nazi Germany, which is why pundits were not surprised at all.

The formation of the UPC (Union of the Populations of the Camerouns) in French Cameroun in 1946 and the birth of sister union-nationalist (civic-nationalist) parties in British Cameroons highlighted the seriousness of the former Kamerunians to work together to build a "New Cameroon". By 1955, the UPC commanded more than 80% of popular support in French

Cameroun.

So pundits considered it foolhardy when the French government issued a decree banning the UPC on July 13, 1955, in French Cameroons, a strategic act that was followed by the party's ban in British Cameroons three years later on the same fabricated charges of inciting violence and for being communists. These coordinated moves by Africa's two foremost colonial masters at the time were supposed to spell disaster for the dream held by Cameroon's leaders. Many Cameroonians saw nothing but duplicity and hypocrisy in the moves, wondering whether the freedom they had assisted the Free French Forces to achieve for France and its citizens was a special right or privilege meant for "White People" only.

When in 1956, the UPC resorted to a partisan war of liberation from French rule, it was a belated move to confront France after failing to resolve the ban in a peaceful manner. That war would end with the defeat of the UPC in 1970, a defeat that came with the assassinations and execution of the party's successive heads in 1958, 1960 and 1971, i.e., the deaths of Ruben Um Nyobe, Dr. Felix Moumie and Ernest Ouandie respectively. It would leave Cameroon entrapped through a French-imposed system rooted in the Colonial Pact France made its puppets sign before allowing their countries to become members of the United Nations Organization by granting these former colonies string-controlled independence.

Despite the period of instability during the country's unsuccessful war of liberation that saw the French Trusteeship masters handing power to those who never asked for or never fought for it (the puppets that constitute the system today), despite the eventual peaceful reunification of British Southern Cameroons with the former French Cameroun, despite Cameroon's agricultural recovery and the discovery of oil in the

1970s that saw the country emerge as Africa's eight largest economy and the world's second fastest growing in the early 1980s, Cameroon is today in a horrible shape.

The Cameroonian economy that was expected to grow twenty times over the next thirty years, i.e., from 1982-2012, barely doubled over that period of time. Everything changed for the worse after Paul Biya was handed power in November 1982 by the first French-installed puppet Cameroonian president Ahmadou Ahidjo. Since then, Cameroon has experienced the biggest proportionate embezzlement of state funds ever recorded in Africa. And the country holds the sad record as the country in Africa that has experienced the worst peacetime impoverishment since 1960.

Today, president Paul Biya is presiding over a nation where more than 80% of its physicians are abroad, where more than 90% of its doctorate degree holders are abroad, where Cameroonians invest abroad more than at home, where Cameroonians are voting against the system with their feet; today, Cameroon's neighbors who before envied its high standards of living and saw it as a place of refuge and opportunities, now find Cameroonians envying them as they forge ahead with a sense of direction while Cameroon lags behind in its spiral towards total, complete and horrifying economic, social and political decay.

People unfamiliar with the Cameroonian situation would be wondering why such an abysmal situation persists. Well; the answer is simple. Cameroon finds itself today in a situation like someone in a quicksand because of the anachronistic system put in place by Gaullist France when General Charles De Gaulle returned to power in 1958 and decided to make France's former colonies and territories members of the United Nations Organization (UNO), while controlling them with transparent or invisible strings this time. French Cameroun and British

Southern Cameroons achieved independence and reunification all right, only for the people to find that the new country is quasi-independent under a broader French template of control variously described as FrancAfrique. This French-imposed system has traumatized, demoralized, divided and dehumanized the Cameroonian people over the years.

The Gaullist system put in place by the elites of the French political establishment has as one of its major objectives the exclusion from Cameroon's political power of the union-nationalists advocating for the reunification and independence of the divided territories of the former German Kamerun, civic nationalists who commanded the support of more than 80% of the populations of both territories of British Cameroons and French Cameroun in the 1950s and 1960s. The current system in Cameroon is a partnership of French imperial interest in Africa (economic and political) otherwise known as FrancAfrique and its Cameroonian collaborators (the renegades and anti-union-nationalists who never opposed and who do not object to France's neo-colonial stranglehold of Cameroon).

The system has been effective in infecting the minds of many Cameroonians, reducing them into a state of hopelessness, in a process that lures them to direct their energy not against the Biya regime and the system, but at their neighbors. The system has successfully elevated corruption and the divide-and-rule strategy into an art—it has promoted the notion of settlers and indigenes, it has encouraged ethno-centrism, tribalism, clannishness, regional jingoism, sectarianism and other forms of division. We see a total and complete absence of strategic or even tactical planning when it comes to the economic and social development of the nation. We see a complete absence of social solidarity.

To compound the division and confusion among the people who reject the Biya regime and the French-imposed system, the so-called opposition leaders these freedom-craving Cameroonians had been looking up to have now been absorbed back into the system, leaving the struggling Cameroonian masses distrustful of politicians in general. Today, the down-trodden Cameroonian people are in a state of political lethargy.

When Paul Biya called for the holding of senate elections in April 2013, eighteen years after his parliament promulgated a law to create one, most Cameroonians thought it would be another charade, as usual. It made no sense for the so-called opposition parties with a semblance of representation in parliament to glorify the charade with their participation. Most Cameroonians knew the system was sustaining these so-called opposition leaders financially and that some of them were in the government, but Cameroonians were not prepared for the extent to which these politicians would go to insult their intelligence. But deals between the ruling party and the opposition were made all right. The electoral masquerade took place and the people saw the ruling party campaigning for the so-called main opposition party (Social Democratic Front—SDF) in some regions of the country, while the SDF in the words of its chairman or president John Fru Ndi "…one good turn deserves another...", openly backed the ruling party, thereby ensuring its victory in other regions of the country.

How could that have happened? Politically-shocked Cameroonians have been asking themselves ever since the open fornication between the ruling party and the so-called opposition political parties in April 2013.

To prevent chaos and ensure a smooth succession, SDF spokes-persons and apologists quip.

"Paul Biya has a deal with the SDF to hand over power to one of its members," some anonymous voices within the SDF echo.

If you ask me, my answer is clear. What was supposed to be a Cameroonian revolution that began on May 26, 1990, became a political comedy played by former members of the French-imposed system or political establishment, a political comedy that has gone full circle. The worldwide wind of change generated by Mikhail Gorbachev's Glasnost and Perestroika that swept away authoritarian systems in Eastern Europe and Africa, and that stirred the vast majority of Cameroonians in the 1990s to risk their lives in the streets demanding political change, was effectively controlled by the system. The desire for change that more than 80% of Cameroonians have has been hijacked by the authoritarian system in Cameroon and the so-called leaders of the opposition. The people got taken for a ride.

The biggest mistake made by Cameroonians was that when the clamor for change began, they followed Cameroonians who had no democratic credentials, people who hardly a year before were in the upper echelons of power in the system, but who at the time claimed they had left the ruling party and now opposed it. All the so-called heads of what the world knows today as the prominent opposition parties in Cameroon (John Fru Ndi of the SDF, Bello Bouba Maigari of the UNDP, Ndam Njoya of the CDU etc.) were members of the ruling party right up to the year 1990, when the system was forced to accept multi-party politics in Cameroon. Like the Pied Piper, these so-called opposition leaders lured freedom-starved Cameroonians into greater despondence and political lethargy. Such a feat was achieved only because Cameroonian liberals, union-nationalists, revolutionaries, democrats and patriots who had always rejected the system, thought these so-called heads of the so-called new opposition, these people who were the first to make the moves to create political parties, shared the vision of the "New Cameroon" that Cameroonians fought, died and voted for, a vision that achieved the land's reunification and independence (though it has never been real because it got usurped by the evil system that today is under the leadership of Paul Biya and his French puppeteers.), but that is yet to realize democracy, freedom, liberalism, progress, justice, equality and development.

False are the statements by members of the compromised opposition that had they not openly embraced the Biya regime and the system, chaos would have ensue in Cameroon incase Biya exited the political scene. There is no truth in the statement because the system in Cameroon is authoritarian, not autocratic.

Authoritarian regimes are usually coated with a sublime idea that could be political (Stalinism/Marxism/Communism, Fascism etc.), that could be religious (Iranian and Taliban theocracy etc.) or that could be an interest arrangement (FrancAfrique). in Cameroon, the system is built around preventing those who believe in the Cameroonian struggle (the union-nationalists, otherwise called the Kamerunists) from attaining power.

The system in Cameroon is a collection of individual interest groups, bringing together the propagators of French neo-colonialism and their Cameroonian collaborators. Paul Biya is the head of the collaborationists. And in many ways, he has been acting over the years as an absentee president. Meanwhile, the state has been functioning zombie-like during his quasi-presence. As a matter of fact, even though the mortifying arrangement suited the interest of the puppeteers and the beneficiaries of the system, it exposed the system to popular uprisings since that means the beneficiaries of the system are not clearly or functionally organized. With the advent of social media, globalization, the maturity of post-independence generations that never benefited from the system; and with the soldiers of the 1990s phase of the struggle dissociating themselves from the so-called opposition leaders, the authoritarian system now finds itself even more vulnerable.

The authoritarian system would be faced by a new political force that never associated itself with the system, a new political force that embodies the spirit of the century old struggle for the "NEW KAMERUN" or "NEW CAMEROON" that confronted German colonial control, stood up to French duplicity in the land in a war that decimated more than half a million of its supporters; the authoritarian system would be faced by a new force that embraces the legacy of those who fought, died and voted for the independence and reunification of Cameroon, a new force that rejects all the values of the system that the French political mafia over Africa put in place in their game plan to control the destiny of Cameroon, a six-decade old evil system that can only lead the country to abyss.

Now, as the open and hidden collaborators of the system openly embrace one another (the ruling party and the so-called heads of the so-called opposition parties) starting with the recent senatorial charade where the so-called principal opposition—the Social Democratic Front (SDF) and the party of Paul Biya—Cameroon People's Democratic Movement (CPDM) supported each other's aspirations in agreed-upon provinces with guaranteed votes from party members, the system is encouraging the creation of elite groups of beneficiaries who see or think that their political and economic survival rests only in a continuation or sustenance of the system. We are observing the evolvement of a system that is shedding any pretense of limited political pluralism; we are observing the entrenchment of a system that openly views the people as its number one enemy. Such a system then becomes autocratic.

In a nutshell, Cameroon's so-called opposition political parties that are in symbiosis with the authoritarian system are aiding the system in its gradual transition into an autocratic system, thereby ensuring its survival in a morphed form. The rapidly changing system needs a strong man to be truly autocratic. This would be someone who has hands on the job to act as the president, someone who the French puppeteers would like to portray as the benevolent despot.

As Egyptian writer Alaa Al Aswany said, "The concept of the benevolent dictator, just like the concepts of the noble thief or the honest whore, is no more than a meaningless fantasy."

It is the place of post-independence Cameroonians to reject whatever farce the system comes up with as change whenever power passes down to the generation after Paul Biya. By absorbing former members of his party who for decades identified with the opposition, Biya is trying to give Cameroonians and the rest of the world the impression that Cameroon's opposition is in sync with his vision for the political evolution of Cameroon. Unfortunately, the system does not intend to let the majority of Cameroonians participate or have a say in Cameroon's political development or evolution.

The New Cameroon will be founded. Not by beneficiaries of the system (past and present) but by those who have always rejected it as an evil system that has been leading Cameroon into abyss.

But then, in founding the New Cameroon, patriotic, honest, democratic, unbiased and progressive minded Cameroonians would have to reconcile a country where:

- the system made sure that most of its historic figures who dedicated their lives and even died for the cause for Cameroon's reunification and independence got killed and buried like dogs at home and abroad,
- the bodies of some of these historic figures that got buried abroad are missing,
- a few of the historic figures who thought they could contribute in nation-building got sidelined, cowed and humiliated by the system,

- its first head of state died and is buried abroad,
- and where the people have been insulted for more than five decades by the regimes of Ahmadou Ahidjo and Paul Biya through an imposed minority system that sowed the seeds of division, corruption, mediocrity, fear and despondence that are haunting Cameroon today.

The ideas and ideals of the New Cameroon hatched by the country's historic civic-nationalists and developed over the years by post-independence union-nationalists is Cameroon's only bargain with the future. It is the only nucleus around which Cameroon can reconcile with its turbulent past; it is the nucleus that all the strata of Cameroonian society can connect to in the process of nation building; it is the only nucleus around which a free, democratic, liberal, fair and prosperous Cameroon can be built. The New Cameroon would lead the country in taking its merited place in the central African region, Africa as a whole, and the world at large. That would be possible only if we confine the legacies of the Ahidjo/Biya regimes and the suffocating French-imposed system to the dustbin of history.

Janvier Tchouteu   06/04/2013

Glossary

Adamawa

The southernmost province that was carved out of the former Grand North Province. It is a plateau region.

Akonolinga

A town in the Center Region. It is also the capital of the Nyong and Nfomou Division.

Akum

A Ngemba settlement 9 miles from Bamenda along the Bafoussam-Bamenda road. It is also a traditional Ngemba kingdom and the dialect of the people there.

Ambam

A town in the South Region. It is a sub-divisional capital in Ntem Division.

Ashia

Word used by both English and French-speaking Cameroonians to

	express sympathy, condolence, consolation, encouragement, compassion, harmony, understanding, agreement, thankfulness, and caution.
Bafang	The capital of Upper Nkam Division and a Bamileké kingdom in the West Region.
Bafaw	The principal ethnic group in the area that comprises the Kumba municipality. It is part of the larger Bantu group.
Bafedja	A settlement and Bamileké kingdom in the Nde or Banganté Division, West Region.
Bafoussam	The capital of the West Region and Mifi Division. Also a traditional Bamileké kingdom.
Bafut	A settlement and traditional Ngemba kingdom about 18 miles from Bamenda in the Northwest Region.
Bakweri	The principal ethnic group in the Fako Division, which is located in the Southwest Region. The Bakwerians are Bantu speaking of the Sawabantu

subgroup.

Balengou — Bamileké settlement and kingdom in the Nde Division, West Region.

Bali — A Chamba settlement and kingdom about 18 miles north of Bamenda, in the Northwest Region.

Bamena — Bamileké settlement and kingdom in the Nde Division, West Region.

Bambili — A settlement and Ngemba kingdom about 9 miles north of Bamenda in the Northwest Region.

Bambui — A Ngemba settlement and kingdom about 6 miles north of Bamenda in the Northwest Region.

Bamenda — The capital of the Northwest Region and Mezam Division.

Bamendjou — Bamileké settlement and kingdom in the Mifi Division, West Region.

Bami (Bamileké) — Diminutive of Bamileké.

Bamileké (Bami) — The most populous semi-Bantu ethnicity and the principal ethnic group in Cameroon. It is also their mother tongue.

Bamilekéland
The western half of the West Region, with fringes in the Northwest and Southwest Regions. It comprises five administrative divisions, about ninety traditional kingdoms, and eleven dialectical groupings.

Bamoun
A semi-Bantu ethnicity and one of the principal ethnic groups in Cameroon. Also their mother tongue.

Bamounland
The Eastern half of the Western province.

Bandekop
A Bamileké settlement and kingdom in Mifi Division, West Region.

Banganté
The largest Bamileké kingdom, the capital of Nde Division, its former name. Found in the West Region.

Bangou
A Bamileké settlement and kingdom in the Upper Nkam Division, West Region.

Bangoua
Bamileké settlement and kingdom in Nde Division, West Region.

Bangoulap — Bamileké settlement and kingdom in Nde Division, West Region.

Bantu — A Large group of Negroid peoples of Central, South, and East Africa that inhabits the forests of the Southwest, Littoral, Center, South, and East Regions of Cameroon. Also the largest constituent of the Negroid or Black race.

Bassa — The principal ethnic group in the Littoral Region. It is Bantu speaking. Also found in the Center Region of Cameroon.

Batoufam — Bamileké kingdom in the Mifi Division, West Region.

Bawok (Bahouok, Bahouoc) — Bamileké kingdoms speaking the Medumba dialects, found in the West and Northwest Regions. The principal ones are:

- Bawok-Banganté or Banganté-Bawok is a traditional Bamileké kingdom found in the Banganté subdivision, Nde Division. Much of the kingdom is located in the city of Banganté. Following a series of strives in the early twentieth century, it lost most of its territory to the surrounding Bamileké kingdoms, with its subjects migrating to other areas in Cameroon and even founding new kingdoms.

- Bawok-Bali or Bali-Bawok: An offshoot of the mother kingdom of Bawok-Banganté, founded in 1907 with the help of the friendly Bali-Nyonga kingdom. It is an enclave in the Bali kingdom (*fondom* or kingdom)

Bayangam   Bamileké settlement and kingdom in the Mifi Division, West Region.

Bazou   Bamileké kingdom in Nde Division, West Region.

Beti   Diminutive of Beti-Pahuin. It is also a subdivision of the Beti-Pahuin group of languages and is broken down further into Ewondo, Eton, Bane, Mbida-Mbane and Mvog-Nyenge.

Beti-Pahuin

Diminuted or shortened to Beti, this group of related peoples constitutes the third principal ethnic group in Cameroon. The ethnic homeland of the Beti-Pahuin people is in the Center and South Regions, with fringes and enclaves in the East Region. They are Bantu-speaking and comprise the following:

- Beti (Ewondo, Bane, Mbida-Mbane, Mvog-Nyenge, and Eton),
- Fang (Fang proper, Ntumu, Mvae, and Okak)
- Bulu (Bulu, Fong, Mvele, Zaman, Yebekanga, Yengono, Yembama, Yelinda, Yesum, and Yekebolo.)
- Smaller tribes or ethnic groups Pahuinised by the Beti-Pahuins such as the Baka, Bamvele, Manguissa, Yekaba, Evuzok, Batchanga (Tsinga), Omvang, Yetude peoples.

	Beti-Pahuin people are also indigenous in Equatorial Guinea, Gabon and The Republic of Congo.
Betiland	The Beti-Pahuin speaking regions of Cameroon (stretches from the southern half of the Center Region, to the central and eastern parts of the South Region and extend as fringes into the Eastern province), Equatorial Guinea (Rio Muni), Gabon (the northern half), The Republic of Congo (the Northwest), and São Tomé and Príncipe.
Biafra	The short-lived Ibo-dominated state that seceded from Nigeria during the 1966–1970 Nigerian Civil War.
Bota	A suburb of Limbe, Fako Division, Southwest Region.
British Cameroons	The western third of the former German Kamerun that fell under British control following the partition of the German colony. It comprised British Northern Cameroons and British Southern Cameroons.
Boumnyebel	A Bassa village in Nyong and Kelle

	Division, Center Region.
British Northern Cameroons	The Northern half of British Cameroons that voted to unite with Nigeria in 1961, following the controversial United Nations plebiscite in the territory.
British Southern Cameroons	The Southern half of British Cameroons. Became part of the Cameroon Federation in 1961 following a plebiscite that resulted in its reunification with the former French Cameroun. It comprises the Northwest and Southwest Regions of Cameroon.
Buea	The capital town of the Southwest Region and former capital of German Kamerun.
Bulu	One of the peoples of the Beti-Fang ethnic group with a homeland in the South Region.
Cameroonian Pidgin	Also called Cameroonian Creole or Kamtok, it is the Pidgin English spoken in Cameron. It has five variants.

CDU (Cameroon Democratic Union). Called *UDC (Union Démocratique du Cameroun)* in French — A political party in Cameroon founded by Adamou Ndam Njoya, a former minister of the Ahmadou Ahidjo regime.

CENER — *(Center National des Etudes et de Recherché)*—Acronym of Cameroon's secret intelligence service (National Center for Studies and Research)—that was changed in 1984 to *Direction Générale de la Recherché Extérieures* (DGRE)—General Directorate for External Research.

Center Region — Central province of Cameroon. Comprises eight divisions.

CNU (Cameroon National Union) called in French UNC *(Union Nationale Camerounaise)* — Party formed in 1966 from the merger of the political parties operating in Cameroon. It was headed by first Cameroonian president Ahmadou Ahidjo.

CPDM (Cameroon People's Democratic Movement), called in French RDPC *(Rassemblement* — The CNU renamed in 1985. This is the party in Cameroon. Its former name (1966-1985) was the Cameroon National Union (UNC), which itself was formed in 1966 by the merger of

Démocratique du Peuple Camerounais)	political parties in Cameroon. Before that, it was called the UC (*Union Camerounaise*)---Cameroonian Union (CU), the former political party founded by Ahmadou Ahidjo, the former President of the Republic of Cameroon. The CPDM/CNU/CU/UC has been the ruling party since the so-called 'independence of Cameroon in 1960. Paul Biya is the party's president.
CU (Cameroonian Union) called in French *UC (Union Camerounaise)*	Party formed by Ahmadou Ahidjo.
Douala	Largest city, economic capital and capital of Wouri division and Littoral Region.
Duala	A Bantu-speaking people of the Sawabantu subgroup, they are the principal ethnic group of the Wouri Division and the Douala area.
East Cameroon	The French-speaking federal unit of Cameroon from 1961–72. It was formed from the former French

Cameroun.

East Region | The Southeastern half of Cameroon. The East Region has four divisions with Bertoua as its capital.

Eton | One of the peoples of the Beti-Fang ethnic group. Found in the Center Region.

Ewondo | One of the peoples of the Beti-Fang group. Found in the Center Region of Cameroon.

Extreme North | A province in the far North of Cameroon. It comprises six divisions.

Free French Forces | These were French and Francophone fighters who continued fighting the axis powers of Germany, Italy, and Japan, even after France surrendered and signed an armistice agreement with Nazi Germany in June 1940. It was formed by General Charles De Gaulle, who was a member of the French cabinet on an official visit to Britain at the time of the surrender. General Charles De Gaulle strongly opposed French capitulation and the armistice signed by the new regime led by Marshall Petain that created the Vichy regime in the South of France, thereby allowing the North of the country to be under German occupation. He urged resistance against German control of France and its collaborationist Vichy puppets. The movement drew recruits mostly from the French empire, especially from French Central Africa, of which French Cameroun was the base at the time, under the new governorship of Jacques Philippe LeClerc. Philippe LeClerc led the Free French Forces' first major victory in the war with the capture in 1941 of Kufra, a town in the then Italian colony of Libya. It incorporated forces of the former Vichy regime in the colonies from 1943 and saw its ranks swollen by Frenchmen after the D-Day landing. The Free French Forces achieved their greatest glory with the liberation of Paris in August 1944, led by the French 2nd Armored Division because it had the least number of blacks in its ranks. By the end of the war, The Free French Movement constituted the fourth largest military force in Europe, fighting against the Axis powers. The right wing political parties in France have been dominated by its members and the ideology of its founder called Gaullism.

FSD (Front Social-Démocrate). The SDF (Social Democratic Front) in French.

The political party that is described as the opposition leader in Cameroon. The SDF is led since its inception on May 26, 1990 by Ni John Fru Ndi.

Fulfulde (Fula, Pulaar, Pular, Peul)

A Sene-Gambian language spoken by the Fulani people.

Fulani (Fulani, Fula, Fellata or Peul)

A mixed Negro-Tuareg people inhabiting the Savannah from Sudan to Sene-Gambia, they comprise three groups namely:

The Mbororo, Bororo, Burure or Abore who are pastoralists.

The Fulanin Gida, Ndoowi'en or Magida, who are fully sedentary communities.

The semi-sedentary Peul people who are agriculturalist and ultimately resume pastoralism, but often form permanent communities.

	Foulanis, Fulanis or Peuls are the second most populous ethnic group in Cameroon. Found mostly in the northern provinces of Adamawa, North and Extreme North. Their language is the lingua franca of this part of Cameroon.
Foumbam	The capital of the Noun Division and the Bamounland. Found in the West Region.
Foumbot	Agricultural settlement in the Noun Division.
French Cameroun	The Eastern two third of the former German Kamerun that fell under the control of the French following the partition of the German colony by Britain and France. It became a French mandatory territory and later trust territory from 1918–1960.
Garoua	The capital of the North Region and Benue Division.
Graffi	Pidgin German word for a grass field. A name often applied collectively to the semi-Bantu peoples of the

Northwest and West Regions of Cameroon.

Graffiland — Cameroonian word for Western High Plateau, Western Highlands, or Bamenda Grassfields. Mountainous grassland region of the Northwest and West Regions of Cameroon. It comprises the Bamilekéland and Bamounland in the south, and the Ngembaland, Chambaland, and Tikarland in the north.

Ibo — One of the four principal ethnic groups of Nigeria. Found in the southeast.

Idenau — A town in Fako Division, Southwest Region.

Kamveu — The local council of notables among the different Bamileké kingdoms.

Koufra (Kufra) — An important but isolated Oasis settlement in the southeastern Libyan desert that was of strategic importance for the North African campaign during the Second World War. Its capture from the Italians by the Free French Forces marked the first major battle

	won by France in the war, thereby boosting General Charles De Gaulle's prestige and the morale of the demoralized anti-Vichy forces.
Koutaba	A settlement in the Bamounland, Noun Division, West Region. Also a major military and air base in Cameroon,
Kumba	The largest city in the Southwest Region and capital of Meme Division. It is located about 70 miles north of Limbe.
KNDP (Cameroon National Democratic Party)	Nationalist party in British Cameroons. It led the campaign that realized the reunification of British Southern Cameroons with former French Cameroun.
Limbe	Former Victoria. It is the capital of Fako Division in the Southwest Region.
Littoral	Coastal province of Cameroon. It consists of four divisions.
Loum	An agricultural town in the Mungo

	Division, in the north of the Littoral Region.
Maguida (Magida)	Name erroneously used for the peoples of the Moslem North that originated from the third group of Fulanis—the Fulanin Gida, comprising the fully sedentary Fulani communities.
Mamfe	The capital of Manyu Division in the Southwest Region.
Manjibo	A Bamoun village in the Noun Division.
Mankon	Mankon is a Ngemba kingdom and part of the city of Bamenda.
Maroua	The capital of the Extreme North Region and Diamare Division.
Mayo Tsanaga	A division in the Extreme North Region of Cameroon.
Mayo Tsava	A division in the Extreme North Region of Cameroon.
Mbengwi	The capital of Momo Division in the Northwest Region.

Mboh	A Bantu-speaking people of the Mungo Division in the Littoral Region, with fringes of their homeland in the Southwest and Western provinces.
Mokolo	Capital of Mayo Tsanaga Division.
Molyko	A suburb of Buea in the Southwest Region.
Mora	The capital of Mayo Tsava Division.
Mutengene	A junction town to Limbe, Buea, and Tiko, in Fako Division, Southwest Region.
Nde	Formerly called Banganté Division. It is found in the West Region of Cameroon.
Ngaoundéré	Capital of the Vina Division and Adamawa Region.
Ngemba	The second most populous peoples of the semi-Bantu group. The Ngemba peoples are found in the northern half of the Cameroon Grassland (Western

Highlands), mostly in the Mezam and Momo Divisions of the Northwest Region. The Ngemba people related dialects.

Ngembaland   The Southwestern part of the Northwest Region that is composed of several traditional kingdoms or fondoms speaking closely related dialects.

Nkongsamba   The capital of the Mungo Division of Cameroon. It is also the largest city in the area.

Nkwen   A traditional Ngemba kingdom and part of the city of Bamenda.

North Region   Central of the Grand North Regions. It comprises four divisions.

Northwest Region   A province from the former Federal unit of West Cameroon and the former territory of British Southern Cameroons. Peopled by semi-Bantu groups of Tikar, Ngemba and Chamba speakers. Their compatriots in the Southwest Region collectively call them 'Graffis'.

NUDP (National Union for Democracy and Progress) Called UNDP *(Union Nationale pour la Démocratie et le Progrès)* in French

A political party in Cameroon founded by Samuel Eboua, a former minister of the regime Ahmadou Ahidjo. Bello Bouba Maigari, a former prime minister of the Biya regime, usurped the leadership of the party and has been its president since 1992.

Nzui-Mantor

Banganté-Bamileké word for the panther or leopard.

OK (One Cameroon)

An offshoot of the UPC after it was also banned in British Cameroons.

Peul

A French term for Fulani borrowed from the Wolof language.

RDPC (Rassemblement Démocratique du Peuple Camerounais), Called CPDM (Cameroon People's Democratic Movement) in English

The party in power in Cameroon. CNU renamed in 1985.

SDF (Social Democratic Front) or

The political party that is described as the opposition leader in Cameroon.

FSD (Front Social-Démocrate) in French — The SDF is led since its inception on May 26, 1990 by Ni John Fru Ndi.

Semi-Bantu — The unique and unrelated peoples in Africa, comprising the Bamileké, Bamoun, Tikar, Ngemba and Chamba peoples.

Sokolo — A suburb in Limbe, Southwest Region.

South Region — Cameroon's southern coastal province. It comprises the three divisions of Ntem, Ocean and Dja and Lobo.

Southwest Region — Southwestern coastal province of Cameroon. It has four divisions. Formerly a part of British Southern Cameroons and the federal unit of West Cameroon.

Tchollire — The capital of Rey Bouba Division in the North Region.

Tiko — A coastal town in Fako Division in the Southwest Region.

Tonga — Bamileké settlement and kingdom in the Nde Division, West Region.

Tuareg	A Berber-speaking people of the Mazigh group inhabiting the central Sahara from Southern Algeria and Tripolitania in Libya, to the middle Niger and the northern borders of Nigeria. They moved to the interior of the Sahara Desert to escape the Arab invasion of North Africa in the 7th and 8th century.
UDC *(Union Démocratique du Cameroun)* or CDU (Cameroon Democratic Union) in English	A political party in Cameroon founded by Adamou Ndam Njoya, former minister of the Ahmadou Ahidjo regime.
UNC (Union Nationale du Cameroun). Called CNU (Cameroon National Union) in English	Party formed in 1966 from the merger of political parties operating in Cameroon. It was headed by the first Cameroonian president Ahmadou Ahidjo.
UNDP (Union Nationale pour la Démocratie et le Progrès) or National Union for Democracy	A political party in Cameroon founded by Samuel Eboua, former minister of the regime Ahmadou Ahidjo. Bello Bouba Maigari, a former prime minister of the Biya regime, usurped

and Progress (NUDP) in English — the leadership of the party and has been its president since 1992.

UPC (Union of the Populations of the Cameroons) — First national and nationalistic party in Cameroon. The historic UPC was formed in 1948. Banned in 1955, it resorted to an armed struggle that continued well into the late 1960s.

Victoria — Former name of Limbe. Was founded in 1857 by missionaries for the settlement of rescued or freed slaves.

West Region — The southern half of the Western Highlands of Cameroon. It is populated by the Bamileké and Bamoun peoples. It is also Cameroon's cultural and agricultural heartland, and is remembered for its historic role as the center of the country's nationalism and liberation struggle against the French Army in the land. It comprises the six divisions of Bamboutous, Menoua, Mifi, Nde, Noun, and Upper Nkam.

Wolowose — Cameroonian word for a whore.

Wum — The capital of Menchum Division in the Northwest Region.

Yaoundé   Cameroon's second largest city and
                           national capital. Also the capital of the
                           Center Region and Nfoundi Division.

MAPS

Cameroon on a map of the world

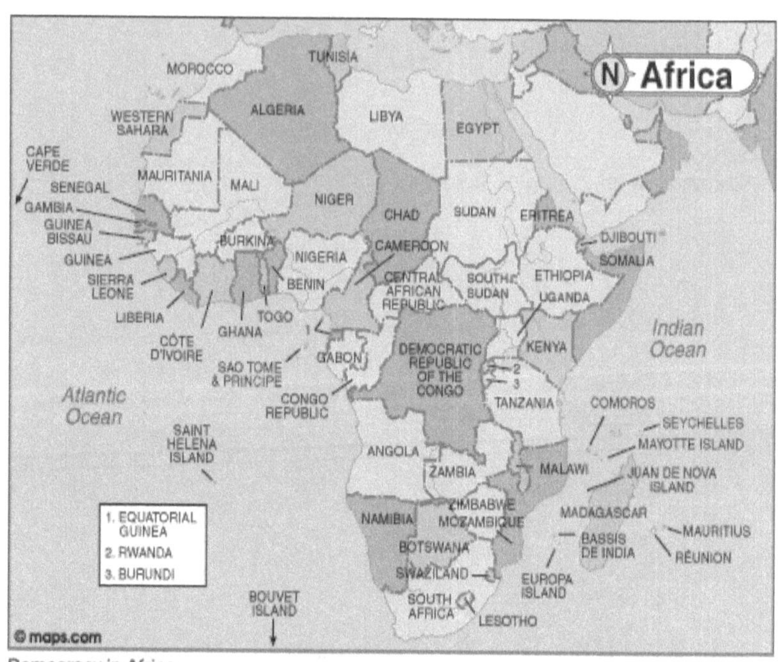

Democracy in Africa

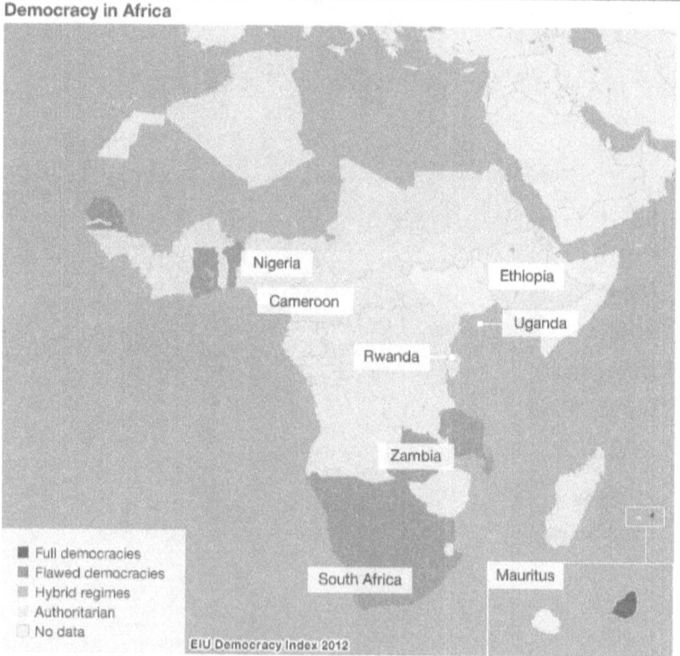

Cameroon over time

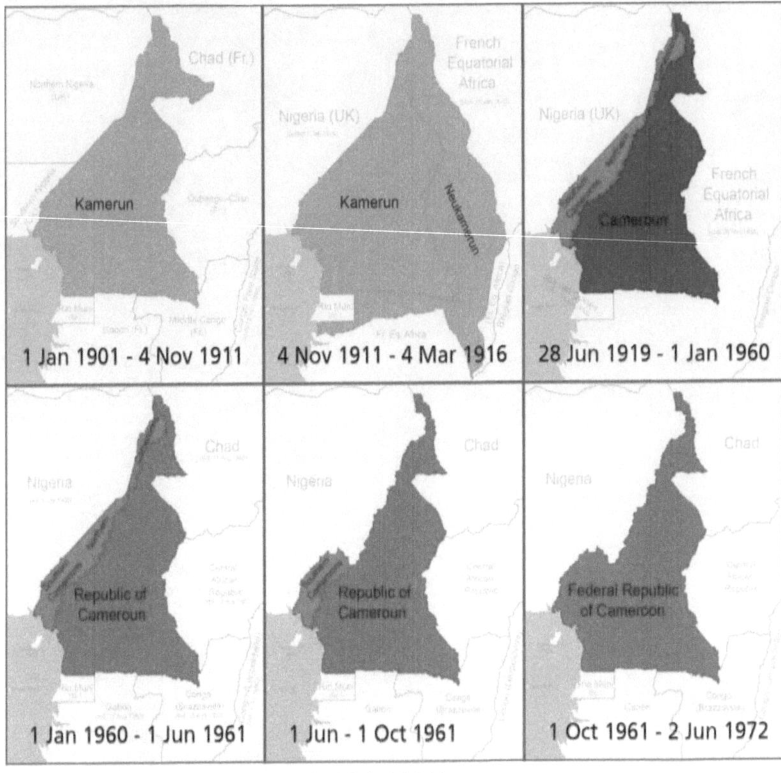

1. German Kamerun (1884-1911)
2. German Kamerun (1911-1916)
3. British Cameroons & French Cameroun: 1916-1960
4. British Cameroons & La Republique du Cameroun (1960-1961)
5. British Southern Cameroons & La Republique du Cameroun (1960-1961)
6. Reunited/Independent Cameroon today.